MOTHER, THREE CHILDREN, A DOG AND BALLOON

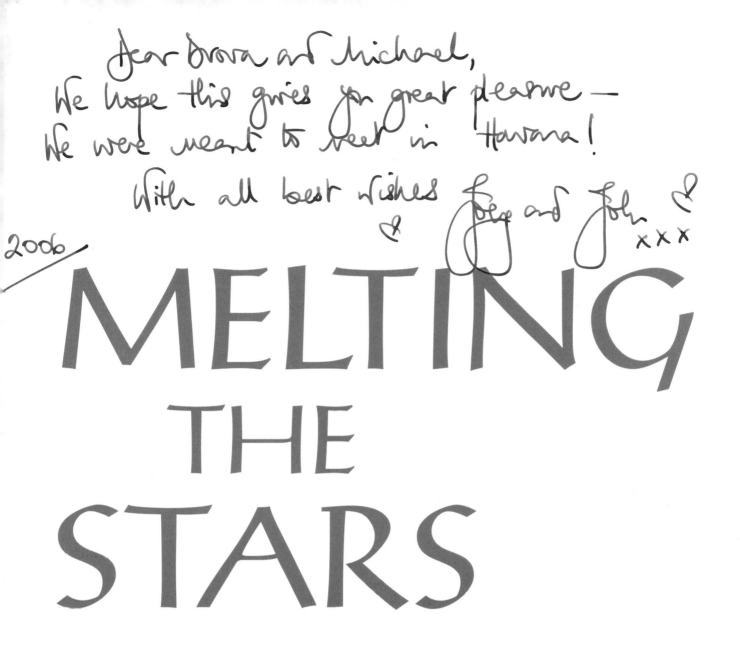

Dear Brona and Michael,
We hope this gives you great pleasure —
We were meant to meet in Havana!
With all best wishes Peg and John
xxx

2006

MELTING THE STARS

An Exhibition by Joey Bieber

For: Hugo, Lark, Kara and Leo *and all those yet to come…*

LOST IN PRAYER

MELTING THE STARS

An Exhibition of Photographs
of the People of Burma by

Joey Bieber

Foreword by Maureen Lipman C.B.E.

BRUNEI GALLERY, SOAS

Previously exhibited under the title
THE BRAVE PEOPLE OF BURMA

PARIS: Terres d'Ailleurs Gallery – October-November 1998
COPENHAGEN: Café Cobra – April-May 2000
ISRAEL: Ort Braude College, Karmiel – November-December 2000

MARGARET BENNETT
SOLICITORS

CAZENOVE   CHRISTIE'S

Acknowledgements

I acknowledge that there may be better photographers than me; more beautiful catalogues may be published, though I doubt it, and other exhibitions may turn out to be more successful than mine. But, *no-one* putting on an exhibition will have benefited from the same degree of direction, help and support that I have been privileged to have received. This I readily acknowledge, adding my huge and heartfelt thanks to a large cast of gifted people. Having lent me their talents, they have without exception given me their friendship, and, above all else, I thank them for that. They are:

Yannick and *Peter Banks*. My dearest friends, for introducing me to Burma in the first place.

Lord Hindlip. Chairman of Christie's, for his staunch and most generous support and for making possible the publication of this catalogue, whose splendid Preface he very kindly wrote. Working together has truly been the greatest of pleasures.

Mary Jane Wilkinson. PA to Lord Hindlip for her ready help and for achieving the impossible in providing almost every question with a wise and practical answer.

Nobby Clarke. Head of Christie's Creative Services, a man of consummate talent, for lending his superb skills to the production of the catalogue and the related printed matter for *Melting the Stars*. The warmth of his support is reflected in the exceptional results of his efforts, which are sincerely admired and very greatly appreciated.

Maureen Lipman. Good friend to me and so many, for her thoughtful Foreword and kind words and the inspiration she provides to me and the millions of others who admire her and her work.

John Hollingworth and *Jacqueline Arrol-Barker*. Of the Brunei Gallery, for the enthusiasm with which they have embraced *Melting the Stars*, and all that they have done, above the call of duty, to ensure its success.

Jeremy Cary. Managing Director of AON Risk Services, for so readily agreeing to sponsor *Melting the Stars* and for his commitment to the exhibition.

James Thompson and *Nick Georgiadis*. For their welcome support in sponsoring *Melting the Stars* on behalf of Cazenoves, and their interest in my work.

Margaret Bennett. Principal of Margaret Bennett Solicitors, for her continuing support for my work and for sponsoring *Melting the Stars*.

Michael Cockerham. My photographic mentor and the expert printer of all the photographs in *Melting the Stars*, for his constant help and professional advice, his devotion to the exhibition from Paris to Copenhagen to Israel and back again to London, and, most importantly, for his friendship to me and my family.

Richard Nathanson. A very special friend, for his particular interest in, and most helpful suggestions about my work, for which I shall always be enormously grateful.

Hugo Bieber. The young man whose skills on the computer have made this exhibition, since its inception in 1998, a practical possibility. I marvel at his talents, my gratitude enriched by pride, as he is my son.

Lark, Kara and *Leo Bieber*. My children, also, who, with their brother, have unfailingly given their support, help and love to this exhibition, making it a genuine family affair.

My Parents. For giving me my first camera aged 6½.

John Bieber. My husband, beloved friend, lens carrier and caption writer, my everything, without whom there would be no stars to melt.

Thank you

Joey Bieber

Contents

Published to accompany the Exhibition MELTING THE STARS held at the Brunei Gallery, SOAS from
12 July to 7 December 2001

Preface © Lord Hindlip

Foreword © Maureen Lipman C.B.E.

Introduction and captions © John Bieber.

All photographs are the copyright of Joey Bieber.

Published by Christie's

ISBN 0 903432 69 2

A catalogue record for this book is available from the British Library

Printed in London by Christie's International Media Division, 21-25 South Lambeth Road, London SW8 1SX.

NUN UNDER AN UMBRELLA

Preface

It is a common sin to express an opinion on a subject or person, or on a whole country, while knowing very little about it, people do it all the time! I try not to, but as the sponsor for this lovely exhibition I have been asked to write this preface, and my views on Burma fall into that category.

Like everyone else, I have read of the sacrifices of Aung San Suu Kyi, and the extraordinary bravery of men like James Mawdsley in their differing quests to bring freedom and democracy to Burma, and shine a light into its darker corners. Hugely impressive as these sacrifices are, they remain at some distance; the photographs of Joey Bieber, however, whose exhibition here at the Brunei Gallery it is my privilege to sponsor, bring Burma and its people into sharp and vivid focus.

Some of the photographs illustrate the poverty and deprivation of the country and the suffering of its citizens, but most demonstrate the extraordinary beauty and serenity of these peace-loving people. Joey Bieber shows us the rivers and temples, the monks, impoverished mothers and their still smiling children, their animals, their whole way of life. She is a wonderful photographer who uses her art for the good of others, in this case the beautiful people of Burma.

Hindlip.

Lord Hindlip

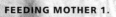

FEEDING MOTHER 1.

Foreword

Joey Bieber's photographs of the people of Burma are the only pictures, aside from those of my children, that I keep permanently displayed in my study at home. Amongst the posters of stage productions which have caused my hair to grey and my crows feet to walk, over 32 years as an actor, I value them for the moments of quiet meditation they give me whenever I glance their way.

They show a kind of poise and acceptance of quiet dignity in a people who have every reason to be very angry. Their history is fraught with domination and exploitation and their democratically elected leader, the gracious and courageous Nobel Prize winner, Aung San Suu Kyi, is one of the world's longest serving political detainees, even though the detention is virtually in her own house. We live in hope that one day the free world will exert the pressure needed to free the people of Burma, and hope is what Joey Bieber's photos are all about. Hope springing eternally...

All of us who know Joey as a wife, mother of 4 and an exuberant enthusiast are particularly proud of her skill, patience and sensitivity as a photographer.

Maureen Lipman

MELTING
THE
STARS

"Human speech is like a cracked kettle on which we tap crude rhythms for bears to dance to, while we long to make music that will melt the stars".

Gustave Flaubert (1821 - 80)

With those lines, tucked away in the pages of Madame Bovary, Flaubert gave expression to the private hopes and aspirations of every human being. Not a person has ever been born who did not just once dream of better things; certainly there was never an artist who did not strive to make that dream come true, to create a vision or a sound, a verse or a tale, that would touch the human soul.

All art seeks to melt the stars, confronting our senses in such a manner that emotions are engaged, thoughts provoked and, for a moment or forever, new and particular feelings are felt.

Of course, all art requires a little magic. A pen, a paint brush, a chisel are not sufficient in themselves, anymore than a camera. All need the sensitive hand of a thinking, feeling, emotional being, someone who will nourish our spirit, as placing their own interpretation on reality, they turn it into art.

Of all art forms, photography is unique. Take away the protection of the camera and the photographer is staring at his or her subject. Photograph a person and, as often as not, the subject will stare back. The result is a two-way passage of emotions, a vital interchange captured and preserved on the face of the subject, for all time.

Whilst writers, painters, sculptors may spend their lives seeking to recreate that interchange, it is only given to photographers actually to catch it. How this is done determines the appeal of the photograph, for each such picture is in essence a study of character, coloured by mood, personality and circumstance, frozen, like a snowflake, as an instant in time.

One particular photograph in this Exhibition exemplifies this to perfection. *Looking out of a Railway Carriage* is a picture of a soldier returning to his unit as his train passes through the former hill station of Kalaw. Pictures of the military are strictly prohibited in Burma, and yet the soldier does not bar the camera or look away. Instead, with a mixture of inquisitiveness, defiance, perhaps incomprehension, he returns the camera's stare. If the lens is an eye, then here is a staring match, a picture worth a thousand words.

Melting the Stars is a collection of such pictures, capturing a way of living that in many ways has not changed for thousands of years. The photographs feature men, women and children still largely ignorant of the ways of the West. All of them are human, built according to the same design, with the same range of emotions, fears, loves, needs and desires as every other human being. They live with great deprivation and hardship, and yet so many evince a gentleness, sustained by an inner strength, that puts us all to shame.

As Joey Bieber's husband and chief lens carrier for the better part of the last twenty five years, I am principal witness to the way in which she captures a moment, a look, a hesitation, a fleeting thought, to bring her subjects to life. From Afghanistan to Bhutan, through S.E. Asia to Cambodia, Nepal, India, Malaysia, Thailand, to Morocco, Egypt, Israel, Jordan, and across Europe and the United States, I have carried her things. Although still in my prime, I have nevertheless acquired a trolley as her bag grows bigger and heavier, swelling, not with equipment, but with little gifts for the people we meet.

For such is this photographer's way. No one is ever diminished by her pictures. However poor or disadvantaged people may be, everyone she photographs retains their dignity.

But taking these pictures was a lot of fun. Burma is an ancient country. Visiting it is like staying in an old, rambling and rather sinister country house. Rules and restrictions abound; hints of menace and suffering surface unexpectedly, but the estate is a place of breathtaking beauty, replete with characters all strangely happy to greet you. Somehow you feel that they should not be there. They have a serenity quite at odds with the harsh inflexibility of your hosts, their simple lifestyle unlike anything you have ever seen. Living without roads or electricity, these people seem to thrive, not just survive, their smiles and sweet, open faces contrasting with the care written on our own, their rich, burnished skin redolent of the perfect golden light bathing the close of an English summer's day.

People are rarely shy of Joey's camera, indeed, her worst problem is combating their eagerness to smile, when she wants to photograph them as they really are. With Burma, however, this was relatively easy, for most of her subjects remained as they were until *after* they were photographed, when, as if on cue, they would then break into the warmest of smiles. So there was no struggle to stop them posing. They were as you see them. Only *Gentle Spirit*, the photograph of the monk descending the steps of Mount Popa, was actually posed, and then only to the extent that Joey missed the monk's first descent and asked him to do it again!

As she said at the opening of this Exhibition in Paris: "You should have seen the pictures I missed!" But those which she got more than adequately portray the ways of an exceptional people, unexpectedly at peace with their traditions and themselves. Inured by a military regime against the temptations of the modern world, they have been preserved from its excesses. Life in the countryside revolves around the monasteries found in almost every village. In the karma of their Buddhism, they are spared the anxieties of our existence. Leading an ox by the light of a flaming torch before the break of the day, the fires from the fishing boats twinkling like stars in the bay, theirs is an existence which has not changed since Biblical times. Without cars, sanitation, domestic appliances, telephones, television, cameras or designer labels, the value of an ox becomes obvious; their humanity shines through.

That humanity is what Joey has caught time and again through her lens, and it is that which melts both the stars on the Burmese flag and those first conjured up by Flaubert.

Art is the communion of all humankind, the one common language we all share. But imagine the subjects of these photographs seeing their images on public display, so many thousands of miles from home. Imagine also if those same people were with us now, exactly as they appear on these walls. How would they react? More to the point, how would we?!

At the end of the day we come back again to humanity, that basic common benevolence that we all share, that can raise the humble, the destitute, the oppressed and forgotten high above the heads of the most privileged, successful, envied and powerful.

Think of this as you look at these pictures.

I hope you enjoy them.

John Bieber

THE LAUGHING BOY

SELLING TANAKA

THE JUMPING CAT

FLOWER SELLER

**CHILDREN ON A WALL
OVERLOOKING THE IRRAWADY**

MOTHER AND CHILD

FISHING BOAT

PORTRAIT OF THE CAT TRAINER

WASHING UP BREAKFAST

NUNS ABOUT TO SING IN BLESSING

SWEEPING UP AT THE "PUMPKIN PAGODA"

SMILING GIRL

LOOKING OUT OF A RAILWAY CARRIAGE

RIVER CHILDREN

AWAITING THE
INAUGURATION OF
NOVICE MONKS

ARDENT PRAYERS

FORTUNE-TELLERS AT A PAGODA

UNFINISHED PAHTODAWGYI PAGODA

PATCHING SACKS IN THE MARKET

CALLIGRAPHY AT MANUA TEMPLE

A FAMILY AT HOME

FEEDING MOTHER II

SHOELESS

BETEL NUT FOR SALE

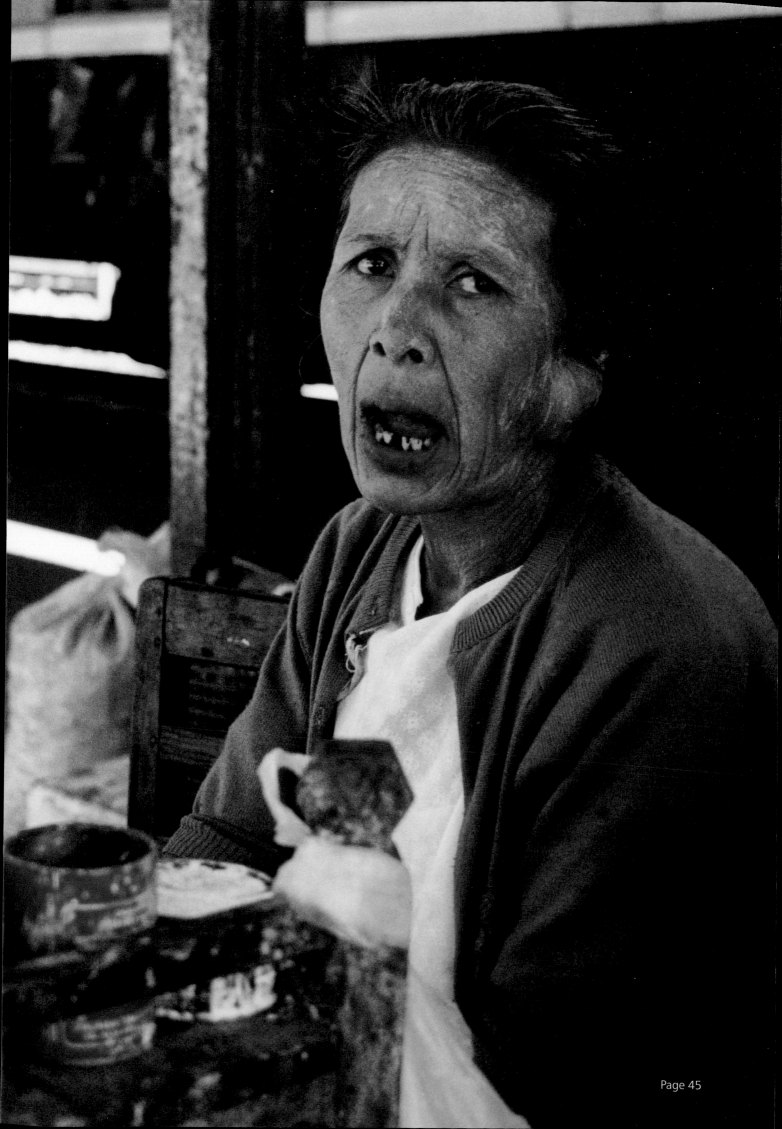

THE PATODAWGYI PAGODA

NOVICE MONKS AT PLAY

ABLUTIONS AT THE AMARAPURA MAHAGENDHAYON MONASTERY

PAGODAS

GENTLE SPIRIT

THREE LAUGHING GIRLS

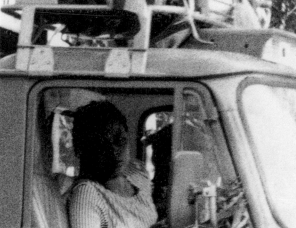

THE BUS HOME

TAKING A BREAK FROM THE FLOATING MARKET

NOVICE NUN AT PRAYER

THREE SISTERS

THREE NUNS ON THEIR WAY TO PRAYERS AT SUNSET

MONKS AT STUDY

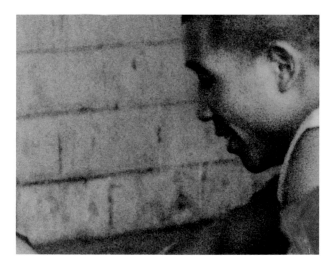

PAINTING THE MONASTERY

WATER BUFFALLO

CURIOSITY

SERVING BREAKFAST

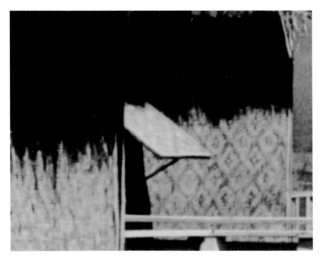

COTTAGE AT THE SHWE IN TA INN

ON THE PLATFORM

OX CART

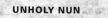

UNHOLY NUN

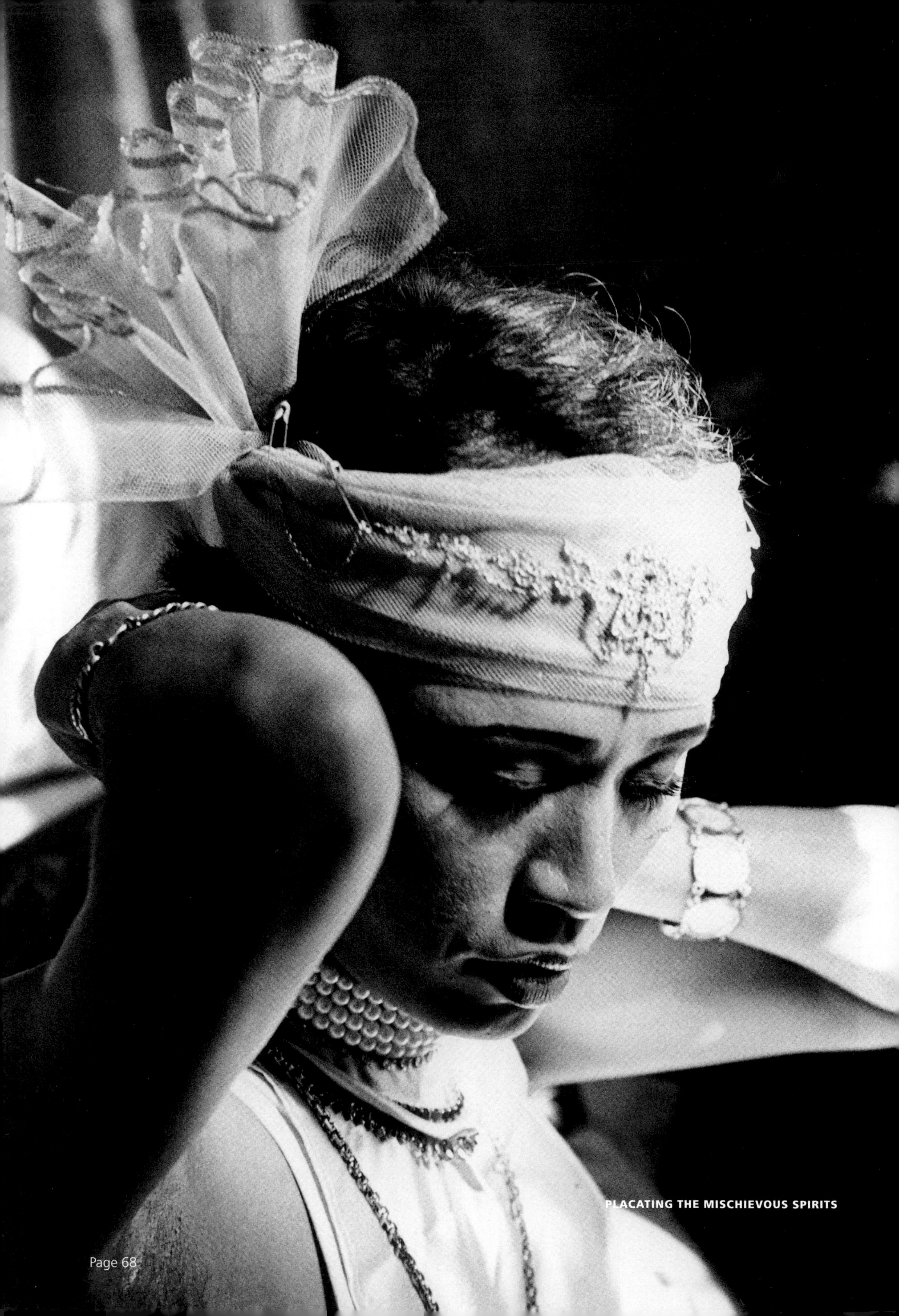

PLACATING THE MISCHIEVOUS SPIRITS

STORAGE DRUMS

THE TODDY MAN

MONK AT THE SHWEDAGON

SETTING SUN

Other Places
Other Faces

BENARES – THE SADHU

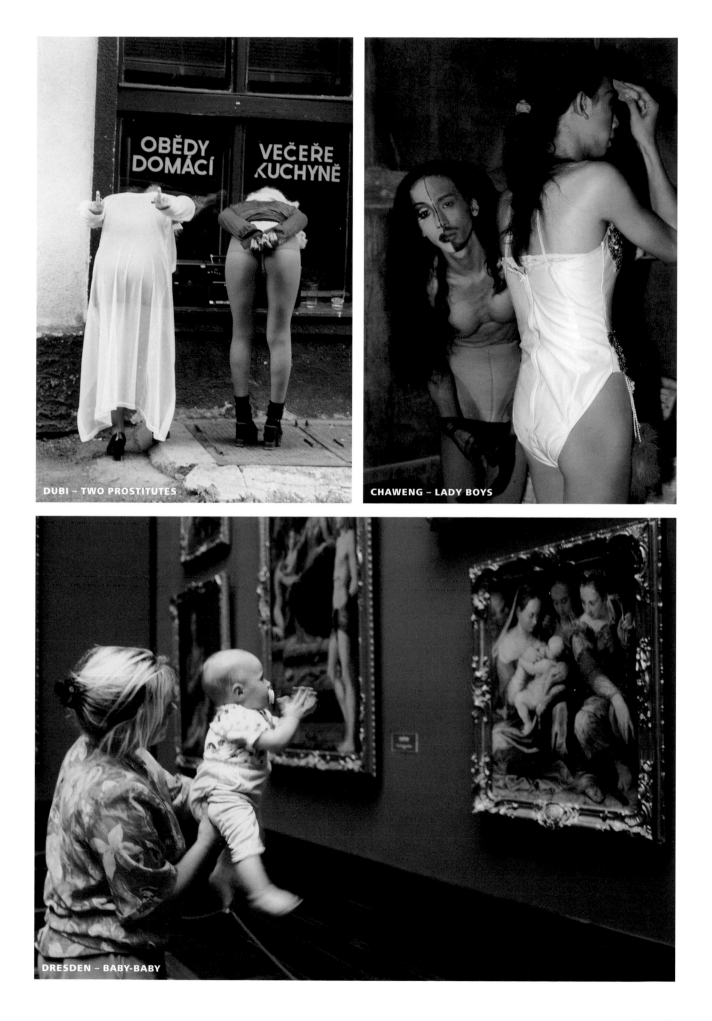

DUBI – TWO PROSTITUTES

CHAWENG – LADY BOYS

DRESDEN – BABY-BABY

SIEM REAP – LIMBLESS MEN

DESERT OF DEATH – BOY WITH GANGRENOUS LEG

A BEND IN THE ROAD – BEMUSED CHILDREN

BENARES – MORNING BATHING

GOING EAST – WOMAN WITH AN INFANT AND CHILD

KABUL – TWO HATTERS

PRAGUE – HARE KRISHNA, KRISHNA HARE

COLOGNE – LOOKING IN AND OUT OF THE WINDOW

JERUSALEM – TAKE MY HAND, HOLD MY HAND

ANGKOR WAR – OLD ENOUGH TO BE A STATUE

CHAWENG – BLUE LADY

ASWAN – BLUE GIRL

PETRA – WATCHING THE TOURISTS

FISHING VILLAGE – NEWCASTLE UNITED

ON THE ROAD TO PONDICHERRY – TEMPLE GUIDE

**PHNOMH PENH –
TWO MONKS AND A MAN ON A MOTORBIBKE**

KANDAHAR – OUTSIDE A KUTCHI VILLAGE

THIMPU – LOCAL DANCERS

BUMTANG – YOUNG GIRL WITH A SMALL CHILD

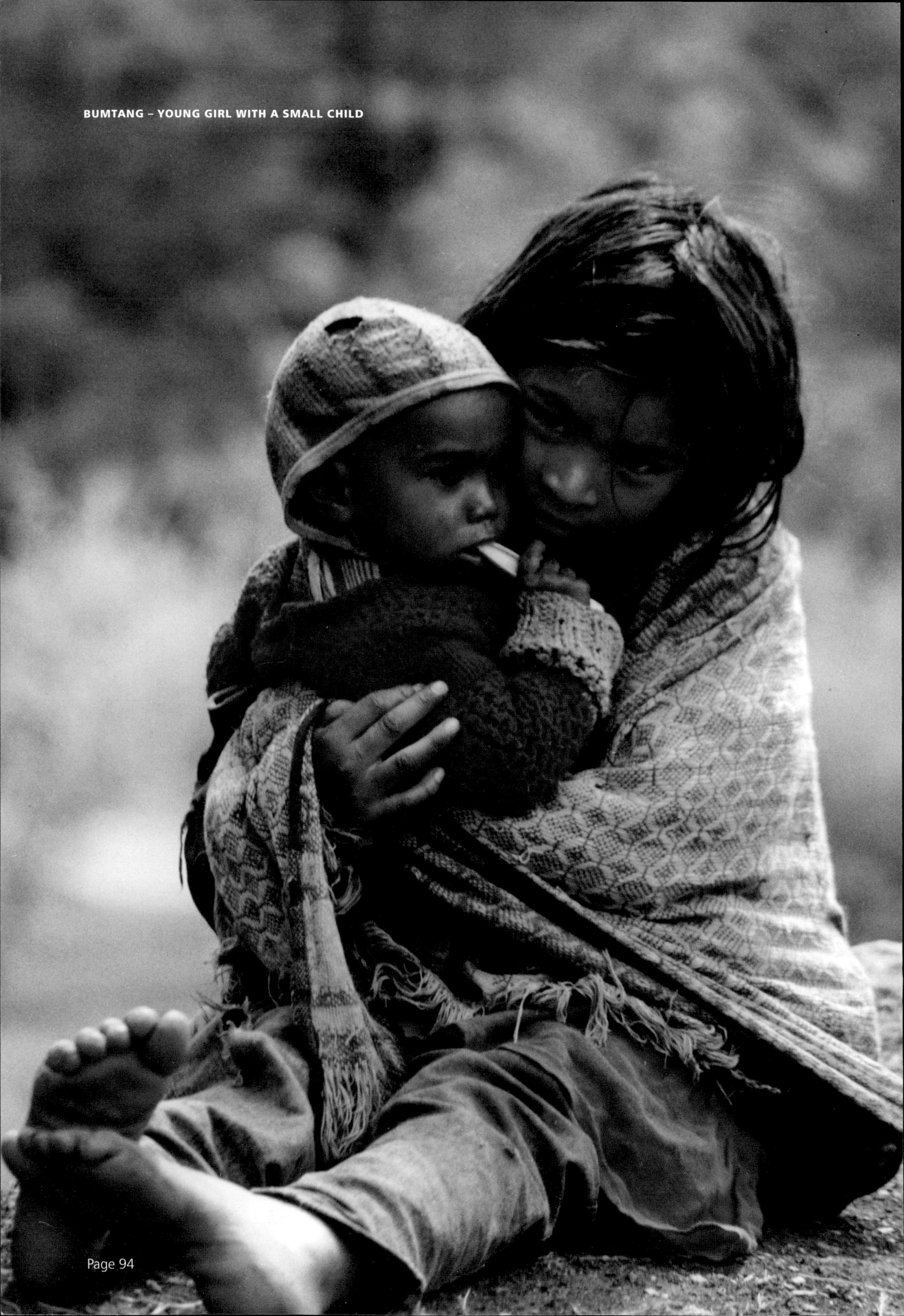

Biography

"There is no greater pleasure than capturing a look,
a glance, a smile and preserving it for all time.
To catch a fleeting moment, to freeze a mood, is to
hold life in your hand."

Born prematurely in Yorkshire, England in 1956, it would cause no surprise to learn that Joey had emerged from her incubator holding a camera, for she has rarely been seen without one, since.

Her home, on a farm set deep in the country, in Sussex, England, may be full of the usual things that fill houses holding four teenage children, a dog, donkeys and a husband, but hers is also crammed full of albums of photographs, recording life on an almost daily basis.

Invariably travelling with her family, Joey has photographed in countries as remote as Bhutan and Afghanistan, picturing life, exotic or mundane, as it is lived. Whether princes or peasants, in Manhattan or Mandalay, we are, all of us, the same, our repertory of feelings identical, and Joey's lens appears to love us all.

This Exhibition originally opened in Paris, in 1998, by HRH Duc d'Orléans, is Joey's first. Having already been shown in Denmark and Israel, it now comes to the magnificent Brunei Gallery in London, which, as part of the School of Oriental and African Studies of London University, has a special interest in Asia.

Educated at various schools in England, Joey graduated from the Sotheby's Fine Arts Course, in 1977. A qualified Montessori teacher, teaching confirmed for her the essential worth of every single human being. It is this which she has gone on to capture on film, endowing her pictures with an almost tangible compassion and warmth.

She is represented by Camera Press.

Sponsors

Aon Limited
Garrod House
Chaldon Road
Caterham
Surrey CR3 5YW
Tel: 01883 340001
Direct: 01883 835401
Direct Fax: 01883 834008
Mobile: 0771 3500301
www.aon.com

CAZENOVE

12 Tokenhouse Yard
London EC2R 7AN
Telephone +44 (0)20 7588 2828
Facsimile +44 (0)20 7606 9205
www.cazenove.com

Cazenove & Co. Ltd is regulated by
The Securities & Futures Authority and
a member of the London Stock Exchange

MARGARET BENNETT

SOLICITORS

**Specialists in divorce
and family law**

*CHARLTON HOUSE
5A BLOOMSBURY SQUARE
LONDON WC1A 2LX
TEL: +44 (0)20 7404 6465
FAX: +44 (0)20 7240 5492
E-MAIL: exclusive@divorce.uk.com*

CHRISTIE'S

Christie, Manson & Woods Ltd.
8 King Street, St. James's, London SW1Y 6QT
tel 44 (0)20 7839 9060 *fax* 44 (0)20 7839 1611
www.christies.com

Index

Front cover
Mount Popa.
MONK WITH FLOWERS.

'Give honour unto Luke Evangelist;
For he it was (the aged legends say)
Who first taught Art to fold her hands and pray.'
Dante Gabriel Rossetti (1828 – 82)
And with folded hands the monk holds his
bouquet.
There are some people in this world whom you
know, on first meeting, to be suffused with
gentleness, goodness, and love; in short, to be
one of the few on the road to enlightenment,
the state of being aspired to by every follower
of Buddha. Mount Popa is a holy mountain.
Its summit is reached by hundreds of steps as
grey as the greyness of the West. And yet a
mass of old blues, deep blues, yellows and
faded greens, along with pinks and burgundies
from the habits of nuns and monks, greet the
eyes and weary legs of those who make it to
the Pagoda at the top. A worthy setting for a
monk with flowers held in folded hands.

Inside front, page 1
On the Road to Mount Popa.
TODDY VILLAGE.

Living alongside a road running between two
famous places makes one into an observer of
existence as life speeds by, never stopping,
just a few hundred yards from your door.
When that door is a blanket across a space in
a makeshift hut, in a village of dust, hidden
behind the trees, anyone stopping becomes
an object of intense curiosity for the entire
village.

Frontispiece
Pagan.
MOTHER, THREE CHILDREN,
A DOG AND BALLOON.

'As is the mother, so is her daughter' – Ezekiel.
What mother has not wished for better things
for her daughter? But exchanging poverty and
deprivation for our world is not the answer for
the smiling mother here. Awaiting the start of
an inauguration ceremony for novice monks
and too poor to dress her children in fine clothes
and makeup to join in the celebrations, this
mother is mother-earth, an example to us all,
but, especially, to her daughter.

Page 4
Taunggyi.
LOST IN PRAYER.

Alone and undisturbed, this monk prayed
silently and intently at the Shwephonebwint
Pagoda on the top of Nwar-Lag-Oh-Thar-Pah-
Taung mountain, his sole movement being his
finger and thumb pulling at his beads. He
stopped only to watch the sun turn red and
drop out of the sky, as if in answer to his
prayers. His face had an other worldliness to
it, that you never see in the West.

Page 8
Mingun.
NUN UNDER AN UMBRELLA.

Her eyes are raised not to Heaven, but to the
tourists passing by to climb the steps to the
top of the Pagoda. Her thoughts are with the
begging bowl beside her. Accompanied by
local giggling children, the tourists ignore her
bowl, intent on keeping their balance on the
way up.

Page 10
Pagan.
FEEDING MOTHER I.

Just as a bird will use its beak to break up a
worm before feeding it to her young, it is said
that kissing began with mothers first chewing
on morsels of food before passing them by
mouth to their infants. One of the most
wonderful things distinguishing human
beings from practically every other animal, is
the possibility of eye contact between mother
and child whilst breastfeeding. Like a kiss, a
prime source of our humanity, the intimacy
thus created continues even when both
mother and child have their eyes closed. In
this picture, mother and child are in their own
shared world, oblivious to the noisy
preparations around them to celebrate the
inauguration of novice monks. But, within
seven or eight years, it will be this child's turn
to become a novice monk. The celebrations
will then be for him, and he will have to say
goodbye to his mother.

Pages 14 and 15

Mandalay.

THE LAUGHING BOY.

Outside the Royal Palace in Mandalay, once known as the Centre of the Universe. Covering two square kilometres, it was originally built in 1857 to house the King. Renamed Fort Dufferin when occupied by the British in 1885, it was seized by the Japanese in 1945, and destroyed later that year when the British bombed it, leaving only the City walls, moat and towers intact. The boy is laughing because the soldiers at the gate refused to be photographed. In the distance is Mandalay Hill.

Page 16

Sagaing.

SELLING TANAKA.

Hardly the Perfume Hall at Harrods, but these logs are the material that tanaka is extracted from, the cosmetic cream worn by the majority of rural women in Burma. Some women mask their entire face in tanaka, acquiring a ghostly appearance, but most opt for a large dollop on each cheek which is surprisingly attractive.

Page 17

Inle Lake.

THE JUMPING CAT.

Yes, the cat did jump through the monk's hands! Standing on 650 teak piers in the middle of the lake, the Jumping Cat Monastery is inhabited by four monks and twenty four cats. The monks train the cats to jump through hoops. Even though the monastery houses a collection of Buddhas brought there for safe keeping when the British sacked Mandalay in the nineteenth century, the cats are its major claim to fame. By fourteen months, they are retired.

Pages 18 and 19

Mount Popa.

FLOWER SELLER.

One of several women selling flowers at the base of the holy mountain, this was a mother of five, who spoke good English. The cream she wears on her cheeks is called Tanaka. Extracted from the bark of a special wood, it protects soft skin from the sun keeping the wearer cool. A pale, creamy yellow, it looks wonderful on the deep, burnt coffee colour skin of the Burmese, but quite insipid on Caucasian cheeks.

Page 20

Mandalay.

CHILDREN ON A WALL OVERLOOKING THE IRRAWADY.

With relatively little schooling, practically everyone in Burma retains skills of making things, long lost in the West. Here, a boy and girl are making a toy out of raffia and thread, which will be sold in the markets of Mandalay. Beyond the wall, women sand miners are carrying, on their heads, baskets of sand dredged from the riverbed, for just one dollar a day. Every cent helps.

Page 21

Pagan.

MOTHER AND CHILD.

Squatting is the preferred mode of repose, especially when time means walking rather than driving, where there are no calls to make or telephones to answer, no supermarkets or convenience food, and life still depends on one's own efforts and the support of family and friends. But family bonding is easier this way than high-powered jobs and child minders.

Pages 22 and 23

Inle Lake.

FISHING BOAT.

Despite its name, meaning 'Little Lake', Inle Lake is 112 kilometres from one end to the other. A community of about two hundred villages, four of which float on the lake itself, the lake is a separate world. The fisherman is a leg-rower. This means he will row his boat with his leg entwined around his oar, leaving his hands free to fish with his unique conical traps.

Page 24

Inle Lake.

PORTRAIT OF THE CAT TRAINER.

It takes a lot of patience to train cats to jump. Looking more like a Roman Senator on the set of Gladiator than a monk, the cat trainer was happy to sit for as long as it took to get this picture. The sun, streaming through the window beside him, provided the only light to the monastery's dark interior. Cats were asleep on the spot where the sunlight hit the floor.

Page 25

Mandalay.

WASHING UP BREAKFAST.

Not exactly complying with Public Heath Requirements, there were as many dogs as washers-up at the Amarapura Mahagendhayon Monastery. But, the monks washing-up did not fight like the dogs who were hungry for scraps. The woman in the background was one of several who helped out and may have donated food to the monastery.

Pages 26 and 27

Sagaing

NUNS ABOUT TO SING IN BLESSING.

A sound quite unlike any other drifted through the early evening peace towards a checkpoint on the way to Sagaing. Following the sound off the road and down the hill again, led to a solitary nun singing hymns in the golden light. She was one of ten nuns living with a pet dog in a compound made of bamboo panels. The nuns broke into a chant of welcome and blessing which took at least one minute to complete.

Page 28

Sagaing.

SWEEPING UP AT THE PUMPKIN PAGODA.

The only hemispherical pagoda in Burma, its vast dome reaches over 50 meters. Engrossed with manipulating two brushes at once, the sweeper was oblivious to the camera, and to the woman nearby with doves, owls and sparrows trapped in a cage. By some curious twist of logic, she was offering to free individual birds in return for payment.

Page 29

Pagan.

SMILING GIRL.

This girl was watching the camera before the camera found her. Amused at the chaos caused by the camera's arrival in a small village, the warmth and openness of her smile is typical of the warm welcome given to strangers.

Pages 30 and 31

Kalaw.

LOOKING OUT OF A RAILWAY CARRIAGE.

Pictures of the military are strictly prohibited in Burma. This soldier, returning to his unit, was intrigued with confronting a camera. If the lens is an eye, then here was a staring match, albeit a brief one, as the train left the station.

Page 32

Mandalay.

RIVER CHILDREN.

When you are young, washing your clothes and yourself can take on a whole new dimension when both are achieved with a swim! These children live on the banks of the Irrawady, a great life-line on which all existence is borne, showing them many sights, though not, perhaps, too many cameras.

Page 33

Pagan.

AWAITING THE INAUGURATION OF NOVICE MONKS.

These girls are dressed in fantastic finery as part of the celebration for the ordination of novice monks. Their faces are fully made up with eye shadow, mascara, rouge and lipstick, their tattered clothes and sandals, discarded for a day.

Pages 34 and 35

Rangoon.

ARDENT PRAYERS.

The Shwedagon Pagoda is the largest Buddhist temple of its kind in the world. 2500 years old, and over one hundred meters in height, the gold encrusted pagoda is set at its top with priceless jewels. A worthy rival to the Pyramids, St Basil's, St Peter's or Temple Mount, the complex dominates the capital city. It is always busy; the bustle of pilgrims, monks, and tourists slowly circuiting the shrines, whilst others are still in worship or meditation. And here, a woman in silence, her prayer more ardent than words, oblivious to the activity around her.

Page 36

Pagan.

FORTUNE-TELLERS AT A PAGODA.

'It is because humanity has never known where it is going that it has been unable to find its way'
Oscar Wilde

All life is directed to the future. Our dreams looking ahead to what is yet to come, our lives unfinished and strangely incomplete, we, too, turn to palm readers and fortune-tellers, many of whom are found in Pagodas. An irresistible fascination to Westerners, they wield a huge influence on pious Buddhists, the course of whose daily existence is often determined by horoscopes and astrologers. Listening to the fortune-tellers words, what must the effigies be thinking?

Page 37

Mingun.

UNFINISHED PAHTODAWGYI PAGODA.

This wonderful relic is all that remains of what had been planned to be the largest pagoda in the world. Begun in 1790 by King Bodawpaya it was intended to rise to 135 meters, but its construction bankrupted the King, who was forced to abandon it in 1813. In 1838, an earthquake damaged the building, which looks all the more mighty for the resultant fissures in its brickwork. Denied access through the magnificent eastern entrance, tourists are taken barefoot by local children up a winding set of steps crudely cut into the side of the structure, for a view of the Irrawady and the surrounding countryside. But a shelter next door contains something of unique interest: the world's largest uncracked bell. Cast for the pagoda it weighs ninety tons, is twelve feet high and has a diameter of over sixteen feet.

Page 38

Taunggyi.

PATCHING SACKS IN THE MARKET.

'Grace is given of God, but knowledge is bought in the market'
Arthur Clough, (1819 – 61)

Extending over many roads and alleys, Taunggyi, the capital of Shan state, has a wonderful daily market attracting traders and customers from various hill tribes in the area, dressed in their own distinctive costumes. Practically anything can be bought in this market which has the best quality merchandise for miles around. The sizzle of bananas and potato pancakes, frying in the next stall, may explain this woman's smile.

Page 39

Pagan.

CALLIGRAPHY AT MANUA TEMPLE.

Here was an opportunity to witness the writing of Burmese script – a series of bubbles and circles set amongst straight lines – on a large scale. An art form in itself, deciphering the language is the key to understanding Burmese culture. Even advertising hoardings are hand painted.

Pages 40 and 41

Mandalay.

A FAMILY AT HOME.

A make-shift bamboo hut on the muddy banks of the Irrawady is home to an extended family. The hut is dismantled in the rainy season when the river swells. Outside, sand-miners dredge the river bottom, water buffalo haul teak logs and heavy trucks get stuck in the mud.

Page 42

Taunggyi.

FEEDING MOTHER II.

Taking a break in the Cheroot factory, where twenty-eight women sit on the floor in apparent silence, making cheroots from 8 am to 5 pm each day. Their target is 1000 a day, for which they are paid the equivalent of US $2. The quality of product is truly impressive, especially as it takes only fifteen or so seconds to make each cheroot. Varying in size from cigarette to cigar length, they are made from a mix of tobacco leaves and wood chips, with a maize filter. The woman in this picture sorted the tobacco leaves into different sizes, keeping her baby in one of the baskets with the sorted leaves.

Page 43

Pagan.

SHOELESS.

Everyone removes their shoes at pagodas, but why do pagodas have benches that are too large for a person's feet to touch the ground? By the banks of the Irrawady, at Nyuang-U, the Shwezigon pagoda contains what is believed to be the frontal bone and a tooth of Buddha, making it one of the holiest sites in the country.

Pages 44 and 45
Kalaw.
BETEL NUT FOR SALE.

A former British hill station nestling amongst the pine forests of the Shan hills, 1300 meters above sea level, Kalaw retains many colonial style buildings. Among these is the railway station, where this picture was taken. The woman is selling betel nut, which is widely enjoyed. Betel nut is the seed of betel palm. First dried in the sun, a small piece is wrapped in a leaf of betel pepper with a pellet of lime. Chewing produces a copious flow of brick-red saliva, which dyes the mouth, lips and gum an orange brown.

Page 46
Amarapura.
THE PATODAWGYI PAGODA.

*'Open the temple gates unto my love,
Open them wide that she may come in.'
Edmund Spenser, (1552 – 99)*
Viewed from the U Bein bridge, the largest teak bridge in the world, over a kilometre long, this pagoda, glistening on the Taungthaman lake, must be one of the most romantic sites in Burma. Built in 1820, it rises in a series of five terraces not far from the old city walls of Amarapura.

Page 47
On the Road to Inle Lake.
NOVICE MONKS AT PLAY.

These novice monks played between the stilts under their monastery like any other boys, delighting in the gift of a few small balloons. Their abbot appeared, the only adult amongst them. They followed him upstairs to a dark room with painted wood, a very large Buddha and a circular window. The room served as half temple, half school room. Sitting on prayer mats on the floor facing Buddha, the young monks began chanting, calling out their verses as loudly as they could, as if competing with each other. As this happened, some were still playing with their balloons.

Pages 48 and 49
Mandalay.
ABLUTIONS AT THE AMARAPURA MAHAGENDHAYON MONASTERY.

Just as children do not expect to see those in authority being silly or having fun, so is it incongruous, having watched them complete their final meal of the day with great solemnity, to find monks fooling around whilst washing themselves at the well.
At 10:30 in the morning, there truly is a time and a season for everything.

Page 50
Pagan.
PAGODAS.

*'Religion is the frozen thought of men out of which they build temples'
Jiddu Krishnamurti*
No other area on earth contains so many pagodas. Dating from the eleventh to thirteenth centuries, a time when Europe was building its greatest Cathedrals, over two thousand Buddhist pagodas are found within an area of 24 square kilometres. Such was the zeal to build these holy structures that the land was denuded of trees to fire the bricks used for building. Centuries later the area remains substantially barren of trees. Five of the Pagodas are bigger than Notre Dame and St Paul's Cathedral.

Page 51
Mount Popa.
GENTLE SPIRIT.

*'That he is gentil that dooth gentil dedis'
Geoffrey Chaucer (1343 – 1400)
The Wife of Bath's Tale.*
Rapidly descending the holy mountain, down hundreds of winding steps, this monk appeared like a vision out of the blue, coming face to face with the photographer, very slowly, going up. As a result she missed his picture, but, speaking English, he readily agreed to go back and come down again, to be photographed. He then blessed her, and went on his way, a feeling, as well as an image, of a gentle spirit left behind him.

Page 52

Mandalay.

THREE LAUGHING GIRLS.

Laughter is a universal language and so is mischief. These girls were running around the reconstructed buildings in the precinct of the Royal Palace. Having been bombed by the British when in Japanese hands at the end of the Second World War, most of the rebuilt buildings stand as facades only, empty of all contents. The guards at the entrance refused to be photographed, but were happy to take the photographer's camera to photograph her.

Page 53

Sagaing.

THE BUS HOME.

A favourite way to travel, double decker lorries always create bustle wherever they arrive. For at each stop people descend on the lorry to sell food. Balanced on the vendor's head, the food is clearly visible to passengers and is always in ample supply.

Page 54

Inle Lake.

TAKING A BREAK FROM THE FLOATING MARKET.

'There is nothing which has yet been contrived by man, by which so much happiness is produced as by a good tavern or inn'
Samuel Johnson (1709 – 84)
Away from the din of traders hawking their goods from flat bottomed boats in the floating market outside, where fruit and vegetables, grown in floating gardens, are sold along with household goods. Boats carrying identical stocks of artefacts will converge on a tourist's boat; keen to make a sale, traders will lower their prices against each other to produce real bargains. No wonder it is time for a beer.

Page 55

Mount Popa.

NOVICE NUN AT PRAYER.

Burma is littered with small shrines at roadsides, in gardens and within temples. Here amongst the bustle of temple life, at the top of Mount Popa, sits a novice nun at prayer. Although very young, the nun is no longer really a child. Like everyone else, she has no surname. There is therefore no evident link between family members. Instead, names are chosen by reference to the day of the week on which a person is born. The nun knows of no other way, but even though the whole country is the same, the psychological effect of this must be significant.

Page 56

Pagan.

THREE SISTERS.

In their best clothes, waiting for the ordination ceremony to begin, when the boys of the village will have their heads shaved, be given robes, and take vows to become novice monks. In a similar ceremony, girls have their ears pierced. Practically every large village has its own monastery, with monks coming out every day with empty begging bowls, to return with them full. At some stage in their lives, even if not for very long, most males become monks, studying Buddhist scriptures and helping the community. Society is all the stronger for that.

Page 57

Mandalay Hill.

THREE NUNS ON THEIR WAY TO PRAYERS AT SUNSET.

Modern cities grow too tall for it to be possible to enjoy sunsets at street level, where people are too busy, anyway, going about their business even to look up at the sky. How different life would be if every city had a special hill or mountain, where people could go each evening to watch the sun turn into a huge red ball before dropping behind the sky line, leaving the evening to the moon. In this picture, shadows lengthen, the lowering sun bathing the world in a warm golden hue, as three nuns hasten along the rising, winding road of hairpin bends that leads to a temple at the summit of Mandalay Hill. There, with prayer flags flapping in the evening breeze, monks fill the air with the words of Buddha recited into a microphone. Pockets of mist rise from the valley floor, and, like a thief, darkness slowly steals across Mandalay.

Page 58

On the Road to Inle Lake.
MONKS AT STUDY.

Now intent on their lessons, it is hard to believe that these are the same novice monks who were playing under the monastery. The figures on the blackboards on the right, record donations received from visiting tourists.

Page 59

Kalaw.
PAINTING THE MONASTERY.

Tawyaw, is a remote Palaung village about ten kilometres from Kalaw. Approached by a long and winding mud track cut across the hills, the brick monastery comes as a surprise amongst the makeshift huts.

Page 60

Mandalay
WATER BUFFALO

Man's ancient partnerships with animals is flourishing in the thick, sticky mud of the banks of the Irrawady. Harnessed together to a large and heavy wooden pole, permitting movement only where directed, these water buffalo enter the river to heave out huge teak logs. Having floated freely from the forests up river, the logs are chained to the centre of the pole as the buffalo strain to haul them to the riverbank. It would be quite impossible to do this job with vehicles. The buffalo never complain, even when the water is up to their eyes.

Page 61

Road to Mount Popa.
CURIOSITY.

There is no finer institution than a family when survival is an issue in life. Families then pull together, with all children responsible for one another, as parents work and continue to produce more offspring. Bonded in this way, brothers and sisters experience things with shared emotions. Five faces but the same curiosity, as they confront four western children, all armed with cameras, who might as well have landed from Mars.

Pages 62 and 63

Mandalay.
SERVING BREAKFAST.

It is 10 am and novice monks are preparing the final meal of the day at the Amarpura Mahagendhayon Monastery, housing over one thousand monks on the outskirts of the city. After this, the monks will not eat again until 5 am the next day. Standing in line for fruit and rice, they eat in silence at long refectory tables. The same food everyday. Enough to nourish their stomachs whilst their minds are miles away.

Page 64

Inle Lake.
COTTAGE AT THE SHWE IN TA INN.

Mosquitoes, no electricity, paper thin walls, every dish a potato, but it was glorious. Built on stilts in the middle of the lake, the Inn hosts entertainments for guests with boats emerging out of the night by the light of flaming torches. Another feature is two sisters, members of the Padaung tribe of the giraffed necked women, who wear up to twenty eight brass rings on their neck, and rings on their arms and legs, originally worn to protect them from tiger bites.

Page 65

Kalaw.
ON THE PLATFORM.

A Burmese version of 'Brief Encounter'. A Palaung couple waiting for the train. Noted for their colourful hats, which they weave themselves, and vary according to marital status, the hat is replaced by a band around the forehead to support the weight of a basket carried on the back.

Page 66

Mingun.

OX CART.

The Tenth Commandment injuncts us from coveting our neighbour's ox. Undemanding, placid, strong, it is easy to see why this should be so. Widely used in rural areas for collecting water, pulling carts and ploughing, the steady plodding ox seems to be pulling all history behind it, its pace attuned to a by-gone age when owning an ox was much to be envied. Indeed, not only do oxen go in reverse, but they are so revered for their steadfast companionship and help in rural life, that many Buddhists either refrain from eating beef altogether, or do not eat beef with rice. Having helped man with his crops, how could man eat the ox together with those crops, later on?

Page 67

Mingun

UNHOLY NUN

'Come pensive nun, devout and pure,
Sober, steadfast and demure'
Milton

Not quite the home counties' image of a stereotypical nun, but a nun, nonetheless. Slightly less than holy, but no doubt a good judge of human kind, this nun with home-made cheroot spends her days awaiting tourists at the entrance to the great white pagoda, her begging bowl never quite empty, but never quite full.

Page 68

Mount Popa.

PLACATING THE MISCHIEVOUS SPIRITS.

This transvestite was part of a group involved in a ceremony to placate the Nats, or mischievous spirits. Debauched dancing, cross-dressing, heavy smoking, lewd singing, the most bizarre rituals are all employed to assuage the Nats, which maintain a significant influence over Burmese people.

Page 69 (top)

Pagan.

STORAGE DRUMS.

Unaware of how awesome the nearby pagodas are to Western eyes, the boy presides over his storage drums at the edge of his village, a statement to Western fashion.

Page 69 (bottom)

On the Road to Mount Popa

THE TODDY MAN

This man is about to collect toddy, a juice extracted from palm trees. After fermentation, toddy becomes highly intoxicating, but it is processed and sold in the form of a confection so sickly sweet that each toddy village could keep a dentist in full employment.

Page 70

Rangoon.

MONK AT THE SHWEDAGON.

Buddhism is rejected by religions as non-theistic philosophy, a science of the mind, and by philosophers as a religion, but through the silence of personal experience, it can, uniquely, serve as a bridge between the two. It is humbling to think of a society where, if only for a while, a majority submit to that silence, when the world at large has never been more voluble. This monk, one of many at the Shwedagon, will have examined and meditated on Buddha's teachings in his quest for inner peace, freeing himself from negative emotions, self-obsession and ignorance that blight so many lives.

Page 71

Irrawady Delta.

SETTING SUN.

As the Irrawady finally runs into the Andaman Sea, and the sun starts its descent, the world begins to look like a chocolate box. The beauty of the delta is breathtaking, the river taking on a new energy as it merges with the sea.

Other Places
Other Faces

Page 72

India

BENARES – THE SADHU

The Hindu religion is one of the oldest surviving religions in the world. Its billion adherents would revere this Sadhu as a holy man. Perhaps his nakedness and floor length hair clothe him with the authority that vestements and ornaments serve to do in Western religion. His wristwatch links him with our times. The Sadhu would be equally at home in any other age.

Page 73 (Top Left)

The Czech Republic

DUBI – TWO PROSTITUTES

The last town before the border with Germany, Dubi has become a living shrine to love, albeit of an instant, transient kind. There is a girl for every man in every truck, car or bus passing through on the way to Germany, their presence on the roadside the best way yet invented to slow traffic flow.

Page 73 (Top Right)

Thailand

CHAWENG – LADY BOYS

Getting ready for the night's performance in one of the many crowded bars these lady boys are far more beautiful than the giggling girls in the other bars. Half man, half woman, the dancer on the left shows how the lady boys have become a third sex, reaching out for a new life that they are unable to find in the old.

Page 73 (Bottom)

Germany

DRESDEN – BABY-BABY

It may not be customary to applaud a painting, but then how often do paintings provide that wonderous sense of euphoric delight that is an infant's first stirring of awareness?

Pages 74-75

Cambodia

SIEM REAP – LIMBLESS MEN

"Now tell us about the war,
And what they fought each
other for,"
Robert Southey (1774-1843)

Cambodia has become a land of amputees. Now, years after the close of hostilities, landmines still remove a foot, an arm, a head, as the nation clears them from its fields and jungles, its roads and tracks, even the ancient temples that bring the tourists in their droves. Existence is harsh enough without being disabled, but the human spirit can astonish those who would look on in horror, by its capacity to fire the victims of misfortune with courage and dignity, to find hope and hold on to it come what may.

Page 76

Afghanistan

DESERT OF DEATH –
BOY WITH GANGRENOUS LEG

The night before this picture was taken, the boy's father had appeared out of the blue as we were making camp for our first night in the desert. Having not heard or seen him come, at first we were alarmed to find him standing over us, scimitar in hand, but then we noticed that his eyes seemed full of fear. Urging us to feel his pulse was his way to tell us of his desperate need for a doctor to treat his son's leg, which was turning gangrenous. A young medical student who was with us, burned the boy's scabs with matches, before bandaging his leg. In gratitude the father fell on his face to Allah; deeply moved, declaring henceforth that she would devote her life to medicine in the Third World, the medical student knelt in prayer to Jesus, whilst we stood up to give thanks to our God.

Page 77

Nepal

**A BEND IN THE ROAD –
BEMUSED CHILDREN**

There is only one road from Kathmandu to the Chinese border. If you drive up it, there is no other way back. As we returned from the border after bathing in hot springs, we entered a village where a road-block forced us to stop. A dead chicken was on the ground, being nibbled by its former friends and family, whilst its apparent owner, accompanied by a crowd, brandished a meat cleaver at our driver, apparently holding him responsible for the chicken's death. Of course there was no evidence, simply the frenzy of one hysterical man. After much ado the hapless driver was forced to hand over some money. We were free to go, but not before some photographs were taken, including this, a pictorial definition of bemusement. How often can a dead chicken be made to earn its keep, when there is no other way home?

Pages 78-79

India

BENARES – MORNING BATHING

If Canaletto had been to Benares, this is how he would have painted it. The Ganges is a a life giving river, but it is hard to imagine the portents of death that hung over its banks as these pilgrims immersed themselves in its holy waters. Funeral boats glided silently by, there was an occasional thud as a skull exploded in a funeral pyre nearby, and yet, true to all that is claimed for the Ganges, the lasting impression was one of ineffable peace.

Page 80

Bhutan

**GOING EAST – WOMAN WITH
AN INFANT AND CHILD**

In a land where the King has four wives (who are sisters) the women in the east of the country, which is four to seven days walk from Thimpu, the capital, have been known to have up to four husbands. The reason is that their men have to go to the mountains, and pastures and forests, to work. Without roads or electricity, it is hard to communicate or get home. Their wives, therefore, travel to them, visiting one husband, moving on to another, bringing clothes and food, receiving support; spiders in the centre of a web.

Page 81

Afghanistan

KABUL – TWO HATTERS

The photographer swapped her jeans for one of these hats, which she promptly presented to the caption-writer, whose youthful image appears in the mirror! This was Chicken Street before the Soviets, before the Civil Wars, the honey-pot attracting wanderers from all over the globe, looking for freedom and adventure, when both could be found.

Page 82

The Czech Republic

**PRAGUE –
HARE KRISHNA, KRISHNA HARE**

Did the Saint really wave at the small procession making its way joyfully and noisily across the Charles Bridge? Were his fingers raised in blessing or was it something else?

Page 83

Germany

**COLOGNE –
LOOKING IN AND OUT OF THE
WINDOW**

The equestrian statue and people with umbrellas inhabit a picture. Are they real or are they an exhibit in the museum? When the girl leaves the staircase, will they move on, and, if they do, will the women on the wall even notice?

Page 84

Israel

**JERUSALEM – TAKE MY HAND,
HOLD MY HAND**

Arab dress and Nike sneakers, within yards of the spot on Mount Moriah where Abraham's hand was held as he was about to sacrifice Isaac. This is Temple Mount, exactly one year before the latest troubles. Holding hands is a very good thing. A sign of affection, a means of guidance, a device to stop your enemy drawing his sword; there is still no better place on earth than Jerusalem for hand holding.

Page 85

Cambodia

**ANGKOR WAT –
OLD ENOUGH TO BE A STATUE**

Extreme old age can produce the most beautiful of faces, when the weight of years is like the breath of a kiss; no more a burden, the soul is at peace with life and death holds no fear. Only then may the body become a statue, a record of a life well lived, an example to all who will look and learn.

Page 86

Thailand

CHAWENG – BLUE LADY

The show must go on even though it is past midnight and there is no-one beyond the lights to entertain, save for a solitary drunk Australian tourist. Being in the spotlight and performing is all some people live for. Others dress up as a form of escape. Here tremendous care is taken to ensure as much glamour as possible. The head-dress is a full metre high. The result is truly astonishing. No-one would ever guess that the Blue Lady is a man.

Page 87

Egypt

ASWAN – BLUE GIRL

This girl lived amongst the dust and rubble of a Nubian Village not far from the Nile but a long way from opportunity. Her family had a television. As she looked out of the window waiting for the occasional tourist, so was her television a window on the world. How else would she have known to greet us with the words "Kevin Keegan"?

Page 88 (Top)

Jordan

PETRA – WATCHING THE TOURISTS

Tourism at many important sites is a family business. What better way for a father to pass on to his son the tricks and secrets of that business, than to sit and watch as the tourists pass by? Observing the tourists, observing the ruins, yields as much information to would-be tourist guides as these ruins, of an ancient pink city, provide to the tourists.

Page 88 (Bottom)

Thailand

**FISHING VILLAGE –
NEWCASTLE UNITED**

Wading ashore amongst the exotic long-tail fishing boats, on the edge of the Andaman Sea, a fisherman with everything to play for.

Page 89 (Top)

India

**ON THE ROAD TO
PONDICHERRY – TEMPLE
GUIDE**

Watching the guide re-enact the tales preserved in carvings on the pillars of his ancient temple, was like going back down the centuries to a time when the gods walked the earth. It was only after printing this picture that it became clear that the emaciated, bent old man was nothing like as old as he had seemed.

Page 89 (Bottom)

Cambodia

**PHNOMH PENH – TWO MONKS
AND A MAN ON A MOTORBIKE**

Three to a motorbike is the preferred way to travel in this most frenetic of capitals, where every adult is a survivor of suffering and atrocity on a scale that defies belief. Only now are the numbers of limbless being exceeded by a new generation as, once again, life holds hands with hope.

Page 90-91

Collage

**MEMBERS OF THE HUMAN
RACE**

I wish I loved the Human Race;
I wish I loved its silly face;
I wish I liked the way it walks;
I wish I liked the way it talks;
And when I'm introduced to one
I wish I thought *What Jolly Fun!*

Sir Walter Raleigh (1861-1922)

Page 92

Afghanistan

**KANDAHAR –
OUTSIDE A KUTCHI VILLAGE**

Ornately dressed, the Kutchi are a nomadic people crossing and re-crossing the country from year to year. Such is their code that belongings may be left on a tree for later collection and, in six or nine months time they will still be there. But that was before the Soviet invasion, the Civil Wars and Taleban. Whatever become of these children who welcomed strangers to their tented village? Was their inheritance of freedom and tradition destined to end with them?

Page 93

Bhutan

THIMPU – LOCAL DANCERS

It was raining heavily when this display of exotic dances was to start. A prayer was recited for the rain to stop. A rainbow appeared against the magenta sky and within a minute the rain was over. Bhutan is like that.

Page 94

Bhutan

**BUMTANG –
YOUNG GIRL WITH A SMALL
CHILD**

What colour would any of us be, if we seldom washed and lived with smokey fires? The child had the darkest of faces but the pinkest of thumbs!

Back cover

*'What this country needs is a really
good five cent cigar'*
Thomas R. Marshall (1854 - 1925)
And it is possible when it only takes wood shavings, cotton waste and a portion of tobacco to make a satisfying smoke! Cigars are a form of statement. But, wherever you may come from, whoever you may be, it is not the cigar but the way you blow out the smoke that makes that statement.